Writing: the team at *Normandie Junior* (Jean-Benoît Durand, Nathalie Lescaille, Estelle Vidard).
Acknowledgement to Marie du Mesnil-Adelée.
Art direction: Gaëlle Queval.
Illustrations : Thérèse Bonté, Sandrine Lemoult (mascot).
Cover: Musée d'Orsay/H. Lewandowski - Thérèse Bonté.
Translation: Claudine Vidard.

2007, Normandie Junior Editions
www.normandie-junior.com
47, place du Général-de-Gaulle
76000 Rouen
All rights reserved

ISBN 978-2-916538-09-9

Act 49-956 of July 16th, 1949 relating to publications for young people.

Printed in France by Lecerf Rouen Offset, Saint-Étienne-du-Rouvray (76)
05-2007 - Copyright 1ˢᵗ published May 2007

Monet and the
Impressionists

Normandie Junior

ÉDITIONS

Table of contents

The Impressionists

On the trail of the Impressionists

Chapter 1

Who were the Impressionists?

More than 150 years ago, some painters revolutionized painting. They left their studios to go and paint in the open air and depict scenes of ordinary life. They have become known as the Impressionists.

Saying NO to academic* art

Most often until the middle of the 19th century, painters depict scenes inspired by religious and mythological themes or great historical events. You have probably seen some of these paintings already: you can almost think they are photos! There are a lot of very precise details, in the folds of clothes for example. At this time a group of young artists criticize this academic painting. Here is their assertion: what is the point of painting scenes of the past while the modern world and daily life provide with topics that are as exciting? This is a revolution indeed!

* Words in colour are explained on page 24.

Musée d'Orsay/H. Lewandowski - Thérèse Bonté

Monet is the most famous of these new painters whose nickname is the Impressionists. He spent most of his life in Normandy, in Le Havre then in Giverny. (See page 16.)

Saying YES to impressions

The Impressionists often paint scenes of daily life but not exclusively. Most importantly, they want to convey the atmosphere of a place with the effects of light. For them, each moment is unique. For example, a landscape by the Seine is never the same whether you watch it at dawn or at sunset. They enjoy depicting wind-blown trees or reflections in the water... To these new artists, realism in the drawing and details is not the point. What is important is to give the impression they experience before nature, the people or the objects they paint.

Musée Marmottan.

Alfred Sisley enjoys depicting the countryside around Paris and the banks of the Seine.

Musée d'Orsay/G. Blot.

Open-air painting

In the 1840s an invention, tubes of coloured paint, makes quite a difference to the lives of artists! Can you imagine that, before then, colours were made by hand with oil and coloured powders? They were stored

A pig's bladder: the ancestor of the tube of paint!

in pigs' bladders which often burst. Because of the tubes they can carry and use easily, the Impressionists leave their studios and set up their easels in the open air. They spend whole days in the Normandy countryside in full sunshine and in the wind.

Colour and light

To convey the impression of the moment, the canvas has to be painted very fast because the movement of the sun makes light different and alters colours. How can they achieve that? The Impressionists create a new technique: they put small strokes of colour next to each other. They often use pure colours and do not mix them. If you study a picture very closely you can make out all these colour "spots". But if you step back, the colours "blend". Magical, isn't it?

Lefranc et Bourgeois

Did the Impressionists only paint landscapes?

No, the Impressionists want to show the whole of society. They paint middle-class people at the Paris Opera or at the restaurant as well as poor people: waitresses, dancers, peasants at work or in their leisure time. And making characters pose in a studio as was fashionable at the time, is out of the question! As in nature, the aim is to catch the fleeting quality of painting from life...

Chapter 2
The Gallery of Paintings

Though different because of their personalities and topics, the Impressionists have one technique in common: they place strokes of colour side by side. It is the viewer's eye which blends them to recreate the depicted object.

Musee Marmottan

This picture is painted by Monet in Le Havre in 1872. It is called Rising Sun Impression. At the time, this picture is considered to be a rough copy or a botched painting! A journalist invents the word "impressionist" to make fun of Monet and his friends. The name has remained.

Musée du Louvre, DAG (fonds d'Orsay) / Jean Schormans.

Musée d'Orsay / H. Lewandowski.

Edgar Degas paints numerous dancing scenes, often from an unusual angle. Unlike most Impressionists, Degas hardly ever works in the open air. He prefers drawing in his studio using his memory but he makes a lot of sketches.

Camille Pissarro is the first Impressionist who removes dark colours such as black from his palette. His pictures are often very bright and consist of small coloured lines close together.

Musée d'Orsay / H. Lewandowski.

Auguste Renoir enjoys depicting pleasant scenes of everyday life, dances for example like here, at the Galette Windmill in Paris. By putting strokes of pale colour on the faces and clothes, he plays with the effects of light created by the foliage.

Chapter 3

The painters of modernity

The Impressionists do not just use an innovating technique. They are never shy of choosing the new trends of the modern world for their themes in the capital city of Paris.

From failure to success

The style of the Impressionists causes a scandal. They are not allowed to exhibit with official painters. A lot of people consider their pictures as mere rough sketches which do not deserve to be shown to the public. So the Impressionists decide to organize their own first exhibition in April 1874. It is a failure. The paintings are not a success and very few are sold. They are compared to the works "of a monkey laying hands on a paint box"! It is only at the end of the 19th century that these new artists begin to be acknowledged by the public thanks to the backing of some great picture dealers. Nowadays, Impressionism is the best-known painting movement in the world.

Musée Marmottan.

Paris is a never-ending source of inspiration with its bridges, its cafés, the Opera, the horse races, the great boulevards (like in this painting by Gustave Caillebotte) or the dance halls...

Learn +
The Industrial Revolution

In the 19th century technical progress changes the lives of the people. Towns get modernized, railways spread out...

The steam engine
It is the most important invention of the Industrial Revolution. Water boils in a coal boiler and produces steam. The steam provides energy which can be used to run machines.

Large factories
Factories are built in regions where coal is plentiful. Workers work hard and are paid very little. Sometimes children from the age of 7 work too. Workers and their families live in overcrowded miserable lodgings near the factories.

Transport
Railways link most of French big cities together. Distances seem shorter. People used to travel on foot or horseback before. Thanks to the train a lot of Parisians go to the countryside on Sundays. Tourism develops.

Modern towns
From 1850 on, towns change. In Paris, many houses are knocked down to give way to great boulevards. The streets are less dirty. Comfort improves with gas lighting, running water... Cafés, theatres and department stores appear.

Wealthy middle-class people
The middle-class people benefit from the industrial progress. They are heads of factories or bank managers. They hold political powers as well.

Learn+

Monet and the cathedral series

Musée Marmottan.

Between 1892 and 1893, Claude Monet completes 30 pictures of Rouen Cathedral. He depicts it in varied conditions: in full sunshine, at dawn, in summer, in winter...

To paint Rouen Cathedral, Monet sits in three different places facing its façade. He paints very fast, up to 14 pictures a day! Then he finishes them in his studio in Giverny, in Eure, where he lives. Monet is not really interested in the architecture of the cathedral. Light is the real topic of his paintings. He tries to catch all its variations, its diversity. "I'm looking for the impossible", he writes. The result is stunning: the façade fills up with blue, yellow, pink or grey hues.

Musée d'Orsay / H. Lewandowski.

This rough sketch depicts Rouen Cathedral. The wavy line reminds us of the effects Monet achieves with his paint.

Musée Marmottan.

14

Monet has chosen to depict a close-up view of the cathedral. The summit of the tower on the left is cut off. He uses the patch of sky at the top of the canvas to create a contrasting effect. Blue, a cold colour, sets off the warm colours that are the pink and the gold yellow of the cathedral.

Musée d'Orsay / H. Lewandowski.

Monet uses a thick layer of paint. If you have a very close look at the picture, you will see "bumps". The unevenness of the canvas is reminiscent of that of carved stone.

Monet does not draw outlines. It is the colour which brings out the relief of the façade.

Musée Marmottan.

In this picture, we do not have a front view of the cathedral but it is seen from a side angle. Right in the middle of the afternoon, it stresses the shadows of the portal and of the stained glass window.

Chapter 4

The Normandy of the Impressionists

From Le Havre to Giverny, passing through Rouen, Trouville or Etretat, the Impressionists are inspired by numerous places in Normandy, at the seaside, in town or in the countryside.

Le Havre and Rouen

In Le Havre, Eugène Boudin makes Monet discover open-air painting. This Norman painter has considerable influence on the Impressionist movement. Jongkind paints with them. Artists such as Pissarro and Monet also paint other big cities in Normandy. The latter completes 30 pictures dedicated to Rouen cathedral!

The Normandy countryside

In his home of Giverny in Eure, Monet becomes enthusiastic about nature and reflections in the water. He paints the boats sailing on the Epte, a nearby river, together with the poplars edging it. He also depicts the gardens in bloom around his house and the neighbouring countryside. For example, he paints a series of haystacks at different seasons. A funny idea, isn't it?

Musée Marmottan.

Monet has a pond dug in the large garden of his house in Giverny, where he grows water lilies. He has painted them several times.

Seaside resorts

Artists such as Caillebotte, Pissarro and Renoir paint famous resorts in Calvados: the picturesque harbour of Trouville and its beach or the great hotels, the Casino and the Broad Walk in Deauville. In Cabourg, Monet depicts the Grand Hotel overlooking the beach and the first sea bathing. Jongkind, Monet, Courbet, Sisley... are inspired by Honfleur. The Côte de Nacre attracts the greatest masters!

The Côte d'Albatre

In the 1880s Monet regularly comes to paint the cliffs on the Channel coast, particularly the ones in Etretat which fascinate him. In 1881 and 1882 he spends months and months painting cliffs around Dieppe. He also paints in Sainte-Adresse near Le Havre, where his aunt lives.

Ian Aspey/Office de Tourisme de Trouville.

The Impressionists are attracted to the town of Trouville.

Did Monet paint throughout his life?

Yes, he did! Claude Monet is born in Paris in 1840. From 1840 to 1858 he lives in Le Havre where, as a teenager, he attends his first art lessons. In the 1860s he goes on studying art in Paris and devotes himself to painting in the open air. From 1871 to 1883 he settles in Argenteuil near Paris. Now rich and famous, he spends the rest of his life in Giverny, a small village in Normandy on the banks of the Seine. Though he has serious problems with his eyes, Monet goes on painting until he dies in 1926. What an artist!

What sort of

If you were a painter, what would your style be?
Realistic like Leonardo da Vinci's, impressionist like
Monet's or cubist like Picasso's?
Do this test to find out!

1 In your opinion, what is the most
important thing in painting?
B Conveying impressions of the
moment.
C Showing an object from its varied
angles.
A Giving the perfect illusion of reality.

2 What do you do when you
do not paint?
C Collage.
A Sculpture.
B Cartoons.

3 Which kind of landscape
do you prefer?
B A river in the sun.
C A stately mountain.
A Rocks and caves.

4 Which is your favourite
school subject?
C Geometry.
A Biology.
B Poetry.

5 Which adjective suits you best?
B Fast.
A Rigorous.
C Rebellious.

6 What is your painting technique?
C Having a circular view of objects.
B Settling down in the open air.
A Drawing plenty of sketches.

painter would you be?

7 What do you like best in life?
B Something changing.
A Something true.
C Something solid.

8 What would you be if you were an animal?
B A small shiny fish.
C A bull.
A An eagle.

9 To decorate your bedroom:
C You hang an African mask on the wall.
B You open your window to see the sky.
A You have a mural painted on the wall.

Answers to the test: For each question, circle the letter corresponding to your answer then count how many A's, B's and C's you have got. Have a look on p.24 to know who you are.

Quiz Time
The Impressionists

Did you read your book thoroughly? To know if you did, answer these questions and check your answers on page 24.

1 Impressionism was born :
A 100 years ago.
B 150 years ago.
C 250 years ago.

2 Before Impressionism, painting is called :
A Academic.
B Modern.
C Funny.

3 What or who do the Impressionists enjoy depicting?
A TV stars.
B Mythological scenes.
C The effects of light.

4 How do the Impressionists paint?
A Very fast, in small strokes.
B Slowly, with a large brush.
C With paint sprays.

5 What does Degas often paint?
A Boxing fights.
B Cliffs in Normandy.
C Dancing scenes.

6 Which symbol of modern times do the Impressionists paint?
A Railways.
B Flying saucers.
C Drive-in cinemas.

7 When do they start being successful?
A At the end of the 18th century.
B At the end of the 19th century.
C At the end of the 20th century.

8 Which painter introduces Monet to open-air painting?
A Eugène Boudin.
B Gustave Caillebotte.
C Berthe Morisot.

9 Where does Monet live at the end of his life?
A At the Grand Hotel in Cabourg.
B In a flat in Paris.
C In his house in Giverny.

10 Which town does Monet paint the cathedral series in?
A Le Havre.
B Rouen.
C Honfleur.

Quiz Answers: see page 24.

This way please !

In Eure

Monet's House and Garden in Giverny

Claude Monet lived for 43 years at his Giverny home. He created an incredible "impressionist" garden with all sorts of brightly coloured flowers and plants. At the end of his life, he painted numerous

pictures on the theme of the water lilies and reflections in the water. Both this garden, which is beautiful in all seasons, and the house can be visited nowadays. The furniture is still the same and the walls are covered with Japanese engravings Monet was particularly fond of.

84, rue Claude-Monet. Tél. 02 32 51 28 21. www.fondation-monet.com

The American Art Museum in Giverny

Works by American painters who came to paint with Monet in Giverny in the 19th century can be seen here. The museum tells the story of American art from 1750 to modern times as well. It stages new exhibitions every year. Have a walk in its garden after the visit!

99, rue Claude-Monet. Tél. 02 32 51 94 65. www.maag.org

In Seine-Maritime

The Museum of Fine Art in Rouen

This museum houses one of the main collections of Impressionist paintings available in museums outside Paris. Admire works by Monet, Sisley, Renoir... The museum also exhibits paintings, drawings, sculptures and artistic objects dating back to the 16th century. Splendid!
Esplanade Marcel-Duchamp.
Tél. 02 35 71 28 40.
www.rouen-musees.com

The Malraux Museum in Le Havre

The collection of Impressionist works displayed here ranks second in France after that of the Orsay Museum! Discover paintings by Boudin, Monet, Renoir, Pissaro, Sisley and works completed between the 16th and the 20th century. This museum is a piece of art in itself with its wide windows overlooking the sea and its futuristic look! *2, boulevard Clemenceau.*
Tél. 02 35 19 62 62. www.ville-lehavre.fr

The Castle Museum in Dieppe

Set up in an old fortress, this museum exhibits works inspired by the sea. Numerous paintings by Impressionist artists can be seen here. They came to work on the Normandy coast, enthralled by the quality of the light in Dieppe: Pissarro, Courbet, Renoir, Dufy, Boudin...
Rue de Chastes. Tél. 02 32 90 12 79.

B. Legros/Château-musée de Dieppe.

On the trail of the Impressionists

Near Le Havre, the small resort of Sainte-Adresse inspired a lot of artists like Monet. In Rouen, have a walk in the historical town centre to see the cathedral he painted so often! In summer, it is lit up so that it looks like it does in Monet's paintings. Etretat and Fécamp, well known for their cliffs, also attracted Impressionist painters.

In Calvados

The Eugène Boudin Museum in Honfleur

Eugène Boudin, a Honfleur paper trader who became an artist, had an influence on the Impressionist movement. He was the one who introduced Monet to open-air painting in Le Havre. He used to divide his time between Honfleur and Trouville-sur-Mer where he enjoyed painting the water and the sky. Visit the museum he created with his friend, painter Louis-Alexandre Dubourg. Then walk along the wharves of the harbour: watercolour painters set up their easels here!
Place Erik-Satie Tél. 02 31 89 54 00.

The Museum of Fine Art in Caen

The main part of its collection deals with French, Italian, Flemish and Dutch artists of the 16th and 17th centuries but Impressionist paintings by Monet, Boudin, Lebourg are also displayed here...
Château de Caen. Tél. 02 31 30 47 70.
www.ville-caen.fr/mba

MBA Caen.

The Impressionists' favourite places

Numerous artists such as Caillebotte have painted well-known resorts in Calvados: the picturesque harbour in Trouville and the great hotels, the Casino and the Broad Walk in Deauville... Monet depicted Cabourg and its Grand Hotel overlooking the sea at the time when sea bathing became fashionable. Boudin, Jongkind and Monet, then Courbet, Sisley, Pissarro and Renoir... stayed in Honfleur. They used to meet at Saint-Siméon Farm, now turned into a 4-star hotel!

Dictionary

Academic (here): showing no originality.

Bladder: a bag-shaped part of the body containing urine.

Convey: give.

Fleeting: not lasting long.

Middle-class: someone who was not a manual worker and who owned riches.

Mythological: related to myths and legends.

Official (here): acknowledged.

Rough sketch: a quickly done drawing.

Quiz Answers

1B ; 2A ; 3C ; 4A ; 5C ; 6A ; 7B ; 8A ; 9C ; 10B.

Test Scores

You have got mostly A's: you would be a realistic painter like Leonardo da Vinci. You could have been a painter in the 16th century at the time of the Renaissance. For you, art is inspired by science. You use your knowledge for the sake of painting. Like Leonardo da Vinci, you think that art makes it possible to create the perfect illusion of reality and express man's genius.

You have got mostly B's: you would be an Impressionist like Monet. In the 19th century you would have joined the group of the Impressionists. When you paint you enjoy depicting impressions of light and movement. Like Monet, you do not mind setting up your easel in the open air. Your works show the beauty of a world where each moment is unique. Very poetical indeed!

You have got mostly C's: you would be a Cubist like Picasso. You paint in the way the Cubists did in the 20th century to depict the changing world. Like Picasso, you do not look at your model from a definite place. You have a circular view of it so that you can see all the sides at once. Your aim is to show objects as they are. Never mind likeness!

Also available:

Normandy TOLD to children — The secrets of **Mont Saint-Michel** — 3,90 €

Normandy TOLD to children — The story of **The Vikings** — 3,90 €

Normandy TOLD to children — **D-Day** — 3,90 €

Normandy TOLD to children — Monet and the **Impressionnists** — 3,90 €

Normandy TOLD to children — The story of **Joan of Arc** — 3,90 €

Discover all our books on www.normandie-junior.com